SHI

A Radical Reading of Chinese Poetry

Yunte Huang

ROOF BOOKS
NEW YORK

ISBN: 0-937804-72-X
Library of Congress Catalog Card No.: 97-75558

Cover design by Deborah Thomas.

Acknowledgment is made for permission by New Directions Publishing Corporation to quote from *The Cantos* and *Cathay*, copyright 1928, 1948 by Ezra Pound.

This book was made possible, in part, by a grant from the New York State Council on the Arts.

Roof Books are published by
Segue Foundation
303 East 8th Street
New York, New York 10009

SHI

CONTENTS

INTRODUCTION

This book is not an attempt to grasp the "essence" of Chinese poetry, nor is it an endeavor to produce an over-polished version of English that claims aesthetic superiority over other works in the same field. It grapples rather with the nature of translation and poetry, and explores poetic issues from the perspective of translation and translation issues from the perspective of poetry. Looking from such a vantage point, translation is no longer able to hide itself in our blind spot; instead, the often-invisible face of translation is being brought to the foreground of poetic texture and the traces of translation's needle work are being exposed to the reader's view. With its agenda hidden, translation is too often a handyman for the metaphysical, mystical, or universal notion of poetry. When emerging from obscurity, translation becomes an ally with poetic material and enacts the wordness of the words. And this book strives to strengthen the alliance between translation and poetry through various textual and conceptual means that I will discuss now.

A passing glance at this book will no doubt yield the impression: annotation is overwhelming. Our modern poet, Marianne Moore, once wrote in "A Note on the Notes," regarding the extensive use of borrowed materials in her own poetry:

> A willingness to satisfy contradictory objections to one's manner of writing might turn one's work into the donkey that finally found itself being carried by its masters, since some readers suggest that quotation-marks are disruptive of pleasant progress; others, that notes to what should be complete are a pedantry or evidence of an insufficiently realized task.

The donkey that is being carried in my book seems to be even heavier than the one in *The Complete Poems of Marianne Moore*, where her sketchy notes are mostly of bibliographical nature. In my book, there are not only notes parallel with the translation text, but also a whole section entitled "**More Explanations**" that comes right after it. But this donkey, I hope, carries more theoretical force than its own weight. By juxtaposing translation text with annotation and even adding more, I mean to challenge a notion of transparency that has for long governed the theory and practice of translation. Such a notion, stemming from a metaphysical ideology that regards language simply as a medium for some extralinguistic "meaning," advocates the erasure of the translator's fingerprints and tends to leave only a clean, uncontaminated (by notes) translation text as a "faithful" rendition of the original. This translation practice, in effect, disguises or ignores the linguistic and cultural particularities within which any poetic work is situated. My provision of extensive annotation in this book is, therefore, a conscious effort to disrupt any "smooth" transaction between different linguistic capitals.

Ezra Pound, whose work has served as a great inspiration and resource for this book, has in consequence become an object of my critique here because of his willful division between what he terms "Luminous Details" and "multitudinous details." To produce a translation that excludes the "multitudinous" annotation would be, to follow Pound, to make it [im]possible for the "Luminous Details" to transcend the linguistic and historical situation of writing. But the contradiction between Pound's volitionist poetics of "Luminous Details" and his poetry that relies heavily on allusion, quotation, paraphrase, and other kinds of annotative textual apparatus that to various degrees deal with the "multitudinous details" is now too commonly known for me to repeat the criticism of it here.

The section entitled **"Radical Translation"** is again my effort to disrupt the smooth transaction of "meaning" by foregrounding the radicals (roots) of Chinese characters. However, the nature of this practice is very different from what Walter Benjamin has characterized as the "literalness" of Hölderlin's translation of Pindar that risks the danger that "the gates of a language thus expanded and modified may slam shut and enclose the translator in silence." The literalness, to Benjamin, is ultimately a property of the "pure language" or the Adamic Language that names things without any mediation. But radicals, as vital components of Chinese characters, are not a representative language that eliminates material mediation. On the contrary, my presenting radicals in translation brings forth exactly the material medium itself. It is true that "the gates of a language" will thus be "expanded and modified," but there is no danger that the gates "may slam shut and enclose the translator in silence" as long as the translator and the reader are well aware that the radicals will loudly and boldly enact the meaning of words, instead of letting the words abstractly, or silently, "express" meaning.

The last section, **"Diagnostic Translation,"** by juxtaposing "What's in English" and "What's in Chinese," aims to bring out what is characteristic of each language that stands as insurmountable blocks to translation. The English list consists mostly of grammatical formations that don't exist in Chinese, such as articles, variations of verbal tenses, affixes, and plural nouns. The Chinese list is basically a list of the radicals taken from the **"Radical Translation"** section, but they are now seen from a new perspective. In the previous section the radicals functioned as vital components of the meaning of the individual characters, whereas here they group together and embody the characteristic of the Chinese language. Let me put it in an analogy: When the ancient people carved words on the mountain cliffs or stone monuments, they chiseled off chips of rocks and left concave marks that have been called "words." But now, instead of musing over the metaphysical absence in those concaves, we are looking at the scattered rock chips to feel the concreteness of the words. And the radicals are just these rock chips or powders that reveal the make-up of the words in a language. Therefore, the "What's in Chinese" list intends to demonstrate not the "essence" but the linguistic features of Chinese, just as the "What's in English" list, however incomplete, attempts to describe the specific mode of English.

Having gone thus far, we have in fact reached a point where translation is no longer confined to its conventional definition. Not only the transference of meaning from one language to another has become a close *reading* of the bone and flesh that physically construct each language, but also the particular mode of translation here, such as radical translation, is meant to be read as English *writing* that is experiencing its own foreignness in the foreign linguistic soil, namely, Chinese. A line such as "*bamboo*-**xiao** *ear*-**sound** *mouth*-**sob**" shouldn't be read simply as an analysis of the radicals in Chinese, but as an English sentence itself. In this sense, both the **"Radical Translation"** and **"Diagnostic Translation"** sections shouldn't be taken as supplements to the "basic" translation that goes before **"More Explanations"**; each of the two sections is in effect a complete translation text of a Chinese poem, a text that brings with it a different notion of translation, writing, and reading. The unconventional versions of translation presented in here, I hope, will unceasingly challenge the "clean, uncontaminated" version produced under the illusion of transparency, a version we can get if we exterminate all the annotation and the other two sections in my book.

But the unconventionality is not solely my own invention. For the idea of "radical translation," I owe a debt to Wai-Lim Yip's *Chinese Poetry* (Berkeley, 1976). Yip, in his introduction, first points to the significance of radicals in translating Chinese poetry, a suggestion which has not been fully carried out in his work. The **"Radical Translation"** section in my book is, therefore, to "radicalize" Yip's radical analysis of Chinese characters and to legitimize it as a method of translation. For the "diagnostic translation," a neologism of my own, I have borrowed the idea from the work of Alton Becker, a linguistic anthropologist. Becker's collaborative essay with Bruce Mannheim in *The Dialogic Emergence of Culture* (Dennis Tedlock and Bruce Mannheim; Chicago, 1995) presents me with a possibility of applying his linguistic anthropological methodology to a comparative study of poetics. The kinship between poetry and anthropology has always been close since Jerome Rothenberg's and Dennis Tedlock's proposition for ethnopoetics. Hence, this book can also be regarded as a continuation of the ethnopoetic conceptualization.

Now, some explanations regarding the textual apparatus applied in this book:

(1) In the **"More Explanations"** section, the Arabic numerals refer to the line number in which the word in question is located (poem title counts as the first line), and the laying out of Chinese lines can be found in the next section;

(2) In **"Radical Translation,"** the words in bold face refer to the so-called literal meaning of the characters, while the italicized words connected by hyphens indicate the radicals in these characters. For instance, in "*bamboo*-**xiao** *ear*-**sound** *mouth*-**sob**," **xiao**, **sound**, and **sob** are literal translation of the Chinese characters, while *bamboo*, *ear*, and *mouth* are radicals in those three characters respectively;

(3) In **"Diagnostic Translation,"** the "What's in English" list refers to the English translation text found in the beginning of each new poem, the one with parallel annotation.

9

And last, I want to express my gratitude to Charles Bernstein and James Sherry. It was in Bernstein's seminar on poetics at SUNY-Buffalo that I did the first experiment on the kind of translation now presented here. And it is Sherry who has provided insightful readings and invaluable editorial advice for the preparation of the manuscript, apart from sending in his ever encouraging and challenging words.

Y. H.
Buffalo, NY
August, 1997

RECOLLECTING CHIN-E

Li Po

A xiao sobs, Chin-E's dream

broken in the Chin Terrace

moon. Chin Terrace moon,

willow hues year after year,

sad parting at Pa Ling.

    Clear Autumn on the

Joy-Jog Plain, the old road

no sound or dust. Sound or

dust, west wind and fading

twilight, stone tablets of the

Han tombs.

Li Po (701-762). He might be not the real author of this poem.

Xiao. A vertical bamboo flute.

Chin-E. A princess of the Chin State. Married to Xiao Shi, a legendary xiao player, who taught her to play xiao to imitate the cry of the phoenix. Her father built them a Phoenix Terrace, where they could play xiao and entertain themselves. Later, Xiao riding on a dragon, Chin-E on a phoenix, they flew away.

Pa Ling. An imperial tomb for Emperor Wen of Han. As a result of its location (by the major route leaving the capital), it was also a popular place for departure, where people would break a willow branch as a token for separation.

Clear Autumn. A festival on September Ninth by lunar calender, when people go sightseeing on the Joy-Jog Plain, a place near Chang'an, the capital of the Tang Dynasty.

憶秦娥
李白

　　簫聲咽，秦娥夢斷秦樓月。　秦樓月，年年柳色，
霸陵傷別。　　　　樂遊原上清秋節，　咸陽古道音塵絕。
音塵絕，西風殘照，漢家陵闕。

[MORE EXPLANATIONS]

2. 簫 (xiao). The upper part, ⺮ , means bamboo, while the lower part is the pronunciation, /hsiao/.

8. 音 or 𤳊 (sound). It etymologically follows 言 or 𠱾 , which means "to speak," or "words." But the latter doesn't have the stroke inside the lower part (口 , mouth), which indicates something coming out of the mouth--"sound." Ezra Pound thinks the lower part of "sound" is sun (⊖) in the character 韶 . Hence the lines in Canto LXXIV:

> in Chi heard Shun's music
> the sharp song with sun under its radiance

8. 塵 or 𡑇 (dust). A horde of deer (鹿) are leaping, stirring up from the ground (土) what is called "dust."

[RADICAL TRANSLATION]

憶秦娥

[Title] *Heart*-**Recollect Chin** *Woman*-**E**

簫聲咽

bamboo-**xiao** *ear*-**sound** *mouth*-**sob**

秦娥夢斷秦樓月

Chin *Woman*-**E** *moon*-**dream** *blade*-**break Chin** *wood*-**terrace moon**

秦樓月

Chin *wood*-**terrace moon**

年年柳色

year year *wood*-**willow color**

霸陵傷別

Pa Ling *man*-**hurt** *bone-blade*-**separation**

樂遊原上清秋節

Happy Walk Plain above *Water*-**Clear** *Plant-Dry*-**Autumn** *bamboo*-**festival**

咸陽古道音塵絕

Xian Yang *ten-mouth*-**old** *walk*-**road** *mouth*-**sound** *deer*-**dust** *silk*-**cut**

音塵絕

mouth-**sound** *deer*-**dust** *silk*-**cut**

西風殘照

west *worm*-**wind handicap** *sun*-**shine**

漢家陵闕

Han *house-pig*-**family tomb** *door*-**tablet**

[DIAGNOSTIC TRANSLATION]

What's in English:	*What's in Chinese:*
A	忄 (heart)
-s (sobs)	女 (woman)
broken ("break")	竹 (bamboo)
the	耳 (ear)
-s (hues, tablets, tombs)	口 (mouth)
-ing (recollecting, parting, fading)	夕 , 月 (moon)
of	斤 , 刀 , 刂 (blade)
	木 (wood)
	人 (man)
	辶 (walk)
	氵 (water)
	禾 (plant)
	火 (fire)
	日 (sun)
	鹿 (deer)
	土 (earth)
	糸 (silk)
	虫 (worm)
	宀 (house)
	豕 (pig)
	門 (gate)

BEAUTY YU

Li Yu

When will the spring flower
and autumn moon end? So
much to recollect! On the little
tower, last night, the east wind
blew again. Unbearable to
look homeward in the
moonlight. Carved railings,
jade steps, should still be
there, only the rosy faces fade!
Asking: How much sorrow
can one have? Just like a river
of spring water flowing east.

*Li Yu (937-978). The last emperor of
the South Tang Dynasty. Captured by
the Sung conquerors and imprisoned
in the North, he wrote nostalgic
poems, including* Beauty Yu,
*reminiscing of his lost kingdom in the
South.*

*Beauty Yu. A tune title, but Yu is also
the name of an ancient beauty.*

*Carved...fade. The poet is imagining
what's happening in his old court.*

虞美人

李煜

春花秋月何時了　往事知多少
小樓咋夜又東風
故國不堪回首月明中
雕欄玉砌應猶在　只是朱顏改
問君能有幾多愁
恰似一江春水向東流

[MORE EXPLANATIONS]

2. 春 or 萅 (spring). 屮屮 is grass. 屯 is the pronunciation of the entire word /chun/. 日 is sun. Grass grows in the spring, thus the association of the word "spring" with grass.

2. 時 (time). The left component is "sun." This character aslo appears in a famous Confucian saying: 學而時習之不亦說乎 (Is it not pleasant to learn with a constant perseverance and application?). Ezra Pound, using his "etymosinological" interpretation, translated this sentence as: "To study with the white wings of time passing/is not that our delight" (*Pisan Cantos*: 74/464-5). Achilles Fang, who once worked closely with Pound and helped the latter's Chinese, explained in his 1958 Harvard Ph.D. dissertation *Materials for the Study of Pound's Cantos*:

> Here "with the white wings of time passing" is strictly Poundian
> "etymosinological" interpretation of 時習 ; he took the second
> ideogram as composed of 羽 (wings) and 白 (white), but the
> latter component appears in the seal-script as 自 . (The composite
> ideogram could then be interpreted as to "use one's 自 own
> wings," i.e., "young birds learning to fly," hence "to practise; be
> familiar with custom," -- Bernhard Karlgren, <u>Analytic Dictionary of</u>

<u>Chinese and Sino-Japanese</u>, No. 781; " 習 is the rapid and frequent motion of the wings of a bird in flying, used for 'to repeat,' 'to practise,'" -- Legge's footnote.) The word 時 "time" cannot here be considered as anything but a temporal adverb modifying the verb 習 .

The misinterpreted character, 習 , also appeared in Robert Duncan's "Effort," a long poem which was lost and then recovered thirty years later among his papers:

> but: pleasant to learn
>
>   this sign　　　　　　　　　習
>   "the rapid and frequent
>   motion of wings" a bird
>   learning to fly;
>   an effort
>
> "of how to enter Heaven?"

The mistakenly stroked Chinese character, among others was "in the manner of Pound but not taken from *The Cantos*."

3. 多少 (many few, i.e. how many, or, how much). It belongs to a group of Chinese words which use two opposite terms to indicate an abstract concept, such as size ("large small"), length ("long short"), weight ("heavy light"). Florence Ayscough, who collaborated with Amy Lowell on *Fir-Flower Tablets: Poems from the Chinese*, made an interesting comment on this linguistic phenomenon:

China is a land of counter-balance. Its people think in terms of compensation, and its philosophy is founded on a belief in the efficacious interaction of two essences which are called Yang and Yin.... The idiomatic speech of everyday life is full of expressions which betray this love of counterpoise. An inquiry is made about size, and the inquirer asks how 'large small' a thing may be -- if length is in question the 'long short' is referred to, and weight is described as 'heavy light.' In writing the fateful letter which decided me to send a cable asking my little dog Yo Fei, whom I had left at the Grass Hut, in Shanghai, be shipped to me in Canada, Mr. Cultivator-of-Bamboo expressed himself in the following words: 'I have been to the Grass Hut, and I have seen your little Yo Fei. You do not know *how many* few are his unwillingness. He *anything, everything* does not like.'

Thus counterpoise and balance are perhaps the most typical of all Chinese characteristics....

5. 首 or 뱀 (head). The lower part is a head; the upper is hair.

回首 literally means "turning back the head," or "look back."

6. 雕 (carve). Originally it is a name of a bird, Diao (vulture). The right component, 隹 is a hieroglyphic bird; the left, 周 means "use mouth." A vulture uses its beak; hence "carve."

9. 向 or 向 (toward). A house with its window open "toward" north.

9. 水 or 川 (water). The other two characters in this last line, 江 (river), and 流 (flow), also use the radical 氵 (water).

[RADICAL TRANSLATION]

虞美人
[Title] **Yu** *Lamb*-**Beauty Man**

春花秋月何時了
grass-sun-**spring** *grass*-**flower** *plant-dry*-**autumn moon** *man*-**what** *sun*-**time end**

往事知多少
footstep-**past matter** *mouth*-**know many few**

小樓咋夜又東風
small *wood*-**tower** *sun*-**last** *moon*-**night again** *sun-tree*-**east** *worm*-**wind**

故國不堪回首月明中
old country not *earth*-**bearable turn-back head**-*hair* **moon** *sun-moon*-**bright middle**

雕欄玉砌應猶在
vulture-**carve** *wood*-**railing jade** *stone-earth-knife*-**cut** *heart*-**should** *dog*-**still there**

只是朱顏改
one-mouth-**only** *sun-straight*-**is red** *head*-**face change**

問君能有幾多愁
mouth-**ask** *mouth-respect*-**you can** *hand-snatch-from-moon*-**have how much** *autumn-heart*-**sorrow**

恰似一江春水向東流
heart-**just** *man*-**like one** *water*-**river** *grass-sun*-**spring water** *window-open*-**toward** *sun-tree*-**east** *water*-**flow**

[DIAGNOSTIC TRANSLATION]

What's in English:	*What's in Chinese:*	
the	羊	(lamb)
much (as different from "many")	人	(man)
blew ("blow")	廿	(grass)
-able (unbearable)	日	(sun)
-ward (homeward)	禾	(plant)
to (as in "to recollect," "to vision")	火	(fire)
-ed (carved)	月 ,夊	(moon)
-s (railings, steps, faces)	彳	(footstep)
-ing (railings, asking, flowing)	口	(mouth)
-y (rosy)	木	(wood)
a	虫	(worm)
	土	(earth)
	首	(head)
	中	(middle)
	隹	(bird)
	門	(door)
	石	(stone)
	刀	(knife)
	心 ,忄	(heart)
	一	(one)
	水 ,氵	(water)
	向	(toward)

SPRING SCENE

Tu Fu

Country ruined, mountains
    and rivers remain
City springs, so deep in
    weeds and woods
Feeling times, tears
    of flowers sprinkle
Hating separation, hearts
    of birds startle
Beacon fires burn for
    three moons
A home-letter worth
    thousands of gold
White hair scratched
    gets scantier
Can hardly hold
    a pin in hat

Tu Fu (712-70). With Li Po, considered as one of the greatest Chinese poets of all time.

City springs. Or "City's spring." In the original, "spring" could be a verb, corresponding to "ruined," or a noun.

Feeling... Hating.... The implied subject(s) could be either flowers/birds or the poetic "I." Ambiguity is used to render empathy.

Three moons. Three months. "Three" in fact indicates "many."

A pin in hat. Ancient Chinese hair style has a top-knot on head, covered by a hat pinned to the knot.

春望
杜甫

國破山河在
城春草木深
感時花濺淚
恨別鳥驚心
烽火連三月
家書抵萬金
白頭搔更短
渾欲不勝簪

[MORE EXPLANATIONS]

1. 望 or 望 (to look far afield). The upper right part, D , is

moon. On the sixteenth day of a lunar month, as the ancient Chinese

believed, the moon is the fullest, and it "looks far afield" at the sun. Amy

Lowell, in *Fir-Flower Tablets*, interestingly renders a famous line of Li Po's,

舉頭望明月(Raise head and look at the bright moon), into:

> *I lift my head and look full at the full moon, the dazzling*
> *moon.*

No matter how awkward the line itself is, Lowell is quite on the money

regarding the "fullness" in 望 .

2. 國 (country). 囗 indicates the walls of a (capital) city or the

boundaries of a territory. Inside, a person (口 , mouth) uses a weapon

(戈 or 𣱚) to defend a territory (一 , earth).

22

3. 草 or 艸 (grass). Grasses grow together; hence two 屮

3. 木 or 朩 (tree). Upper part is branches, middle trunk, lower roots. Another interpretation: ― is "earth"; 人 , roots under earth; when the roots go up, 木 , a tree.

5. 鳥 or 鳥 (bird). A bird with its beak, eye, feather, and claws.

6. 三 (three). ― (one) is the metaphyscial "origin" of the Universe in Taoism. Then it grows into 二 (two), consisted of Yin and Yang. When it goes to 三 (three), it's multiple. Therefore, "three" usually refers to "many."

[RADICAL TRANSLATION]

春望

[Title] *Grass-Sun*-**Spring** *full-moon-look*-**Scene**

國破山河在

person-defending-territory-**country** *stone-skin*-**broken mountain** *water*-**river** *earth*-**remain**

城春草木深

earth-**city** *grass-sun*-**spring** *grass-***sun wood** *water*-**deep**

感時花濺淚

heart-**feel** *sun*-**time** *grass*-**flower** *water*-**sprinkle** *water*-**tear**

恨別鳥驚心

heart-**hate** *bone-blade*-**separation bird** *horse*-**startle heart**

烽火連三月

fire-mountain-**peak fire** *carriage*-**run three moon**

家書抵萬金

house-pig-**family letter** *hand*-**touch ten-thousand gold**

白頭搔更短

eyeball-**white head** *hand*-**scratch**-*flea* *sun*-**more** *arrow*-**short**

渾欲不勝簪

water-**muddy desire not** *meat*-**hold** *bamboo*-**pin**

[DIAGNOSTIC TRANSLATION]

What's in English:

-ed (ruined, scratched)

-s (mountains, rivers, weeds, woods,
   times, tears, flowers, hearts, birds,
   fires, moons, thousands)

-s (springs, gets)

-ing (feeling, hating)

-er (scantier)

-ly (hardly)

a

What's in Chinese:

國　　　(country)

石　　　(stone)

山　　　(mountain)

氵　　　(water)

土　　　(earth)

日　　　(sun)

艹　　　(grass)

木　　　(tree)

小　　，心　(heart)

刂　　　(blade)

鳥　　　(bird)

馬　　　(horse)

火　　　(fire)

車　　　(carriage)

三　　　(three)

月　　　(moon)

家　　　(family)

扌　　　(hand)

竹　　　(bamboo)

NIGHT-MOOR AT
MAPLE BRIDGE

Zhang Ji

moon set, crows caw, frost
    fills the sky
river maples, fishing fires,
    drowsing in sorrow
outside Gusu City, the Cold
    Mountain Temple
at the midnight bell, arrives
    the visitor's boat

*Zhang Ji. A Tang poet (?-780)
famous for this single one poem. Both
Maple Bridge and Cold Mountain
Temple have become hot tourist spots
because of this poem.*

*fishing fires. Lanterns on the fishing
boats.*

*Gusu City. Old name for Suzhou, one
of the most beautiful cities in China.*

the visitor's boat. The poet's boat.

楓橋夜泊
張繼

月落烏啼霜滿天
江楓漁火對愁眠
姑蘇城外寒山寺
夜半鐘聲到客船

26

[MORE EXPLANATIONS]

2. 烏 or 鳥 (crow). Its difference from 鳥 (bird) is the missing stroke in the middle that indicates the eye. Both a crow's body and eyes are black, and not easy to differentiate; hence no "eye" stroke. For the English expression, "bird's-eye view," Chinese also has the same, 鳥瞰 . The Korean poet, Yi Sang (1910-37), has a poem entitled "Crow's-Eye View," which plays with the missing "eye" in the Chinese/Korean character, "bird":

The Wings are Grand but Cannot Fly The Eyes Do Not See Much

(Rothenberg and Joris. *Poems for the Millennium.* Vol. 1.)

2. 啼 (caw). It's a pictophonetic character: the left is a mouth; the right is the sound "ti." Therefore, the character is pronounced as /ti/, and means (bird) caw. To use Pound's "ideogramic" method of reading, we might be able to poetically play out a reminiscence of 啼 (ti) in Itys. Itys was the son of Procne and Tereus in Ovid's *Metamorphosis*. Tereus raped Procne's sister, Philomela, and cut her tongue. Procne revenged her husband by

killing their son and feeding him to Tereus. Philomela, turned into a

nightingale, cried out the name of Itys. So, we have these lines from Pound's

Canto IV:

> *Ityn!*
> *Et ter flebiliter, Ityn, Ityn!*
> *And she went toward the window and cast her down,*
> * "All the while, the while, swallows crying:*
> *Ityn!..."*

3. 魚 or 奐 (fish). 氵 (water) was later added to differentiate

the noun, "fish," from the verb, "fishing."

3. 火 or 火 (fire). A flame with two sparks on the sides. Here it

refers to "lantern."

5. 牛 or 半 (half). 牛 is a bull; 八 indicates "cutting in

half." "Midnight" is therefore 夜半 , cutting a night, like a bull, into

halves.

[RADICAL TRANSLATION]

楓橋夜泊
[Title] *Wood*-**Maple** *Wood*-**Bridge** *Moon*-**Night** *Water*-**Moor**

月落烏啼霜滿天
moon *grass*-**fall crow** *mouth*-**caw** *rain*-**frost** *water*-**fill sky**

江楓漁火對愁眠
water-**river** *wood*-**maple** *water*-**fish fire face** *autumn*-*heart*-**sorrow** *eye*-**sleep**

姑蘇城外寒山寺
Gusu *earth*-**City** *moon*-**outside Cold Mountain** *earth*-**Temple**

夜半鐘聲到客船
moon-**night** *bull*-*cut*-**half** *metal*-**bell** *ear*-**sound** *earth*-**arrive** *house*-**guest boat**

29

[DIAGNOSTIC TRANSLATION]

What's in English:

-s (crows, maples, fires)

-s (fills, arrives)

-ing (fishing, drowsing)

the

What's in Chinese:

木 (wood)

月 　 夕 (moon)

氵 (water)

艹 (grass)

鳥 (crow)

口 (mouth)

雨 (rain)

天 (sky)

魚 (fish)

火 (fire)

心 (heart)

目 (eye)

土 (earth)

寒 (cold)

山 (mountain)

半 (half)

金 (metal)

耳 (ear)

宀 (house)

舟 (boat)

Song on the Youzhou Terrace

Chen Zi-Ang

**Ahead cannot see the past,
behind cannot see the future!
Facing the immense expanse
of heaven and earth, alone
woeful tears run down.**

Chen Zi-Ang (661-702). Once served under the first Chinese empress, Wu Ze-Tian, of Tang Dynasty. Later he fell from grace, and was persecuted to death in prison. This poem embodies his disappointment of the age and his sense of historical emptiness: alone in his time, unable to relate to the sages of the past or of the future.

登幽州臺歌

陳子昂

前不見古人，後不見來者！念天地之悠悠，獨愴然而涕下！

31

[MORE EXPLANATIONS]

* This poem falls into a well-known sub-genre of Chinese poetry: *huai gu* (nostalgia). It is usually written when the poet is standing on a historical site, such as the Youzhou Terrace here, and reaches out imaginatively to certain historical events or characters. While Chen's poem expresses a sense of historical emptiness, another well-known *huai gu* poem, "Chin Yuan Chun: Snow," by Mao Tse-Tung (1896-1976), represents a completely different attitude toward those ancient sages admired by Chen. Mao, as a modern revolutionary (and emperor?), sneered at Chin Shi Huang, Han Wu Ti, Tang Tai Zong, Sung Tai Zu, and Genghis Khan--all the greatest empire-building emperors, for their lack of poetic genius (Mao called them "shit and dirt" in another poem). Mao wrote:

> *This land so rich in beauty*
> *Has made countless heroes bow in homage.*
> *But alas! Chin Huang and Han Wu*
> *Were lacking in literary grace,*
> *And Tang Zong and Sung Zu*
> *Had little poetry in their soul;*
> *And Genghis Khan,*
> *Proud Son of Heaven for a day,*
> *Knew only shooting eagles, bow outstretched.*
> *All are gone!*
> *For the truly great man*
> *Look to this age alone.*

In the last three lines, Mao was apparently saying: "I'm the only true hero in Chinese history." But such an interpretation has never been allowed in the reading of this poem; otherwise people would scream: "Oh, he's such a cock!" Since in the original Chinese, 人物 could mean either a singular "man/woman," or plural "men/women," the orthodox interpretation of the last three lines becomes: Mao was referring to the contemporary revolutionary mass as the true heroes. The fact that some literary scholars actually were jailed or killed, as what happened to Chen Zi-Ang centuries ago, because they interpreted the three lines in the most apparent way, only testifies to a horrible truth: either to *misread* with your head on the shoulder or to *read* with your head in the hand.

2. 前 (ahead). And,

3. 後 (behind). Here we are encountering fundamentally different linguistic conceptions of time in Chinese and English. The Chinese 前 points to the past, i.e. what is ahead of you is the past, while in English "ahead" refers to the future. The Chinese 後 points to the coming, i.e. what is behind you is the future, while in English "behind" refers to the past. So the first sentence could have been translated as "Behind cannot see the past, ahead cannot see the future!" But the orientation of time would have been reversed.

2. 古 (ancient; past). The upper part is "ten"; the lower "mouth." What has been passed down through ten mouths (men, generation) is definitely "ancient."

3. 來 or 来 (coming; future). A wheat plant with four leaves on the sides and sprouts "coming" out from the top.

4. 天 or 天 (heaven). A man stands under a limit (sky). Also,

2. 不 or 不 (not). A bird flies under the limit (sky), i.e. it does "not" touch the ground.

5. 下 (under; down). A smaller object (⊢) "under" a bigger object (—). Its antenym is 上 (above, upper), i.e. a bigger object (⊢) "above" a smaller object (—).

[RADICAL TRANSLATION]

登幽州臺歌

[Title] Climb Youzhou Terrace *mouth*-Song

前不見古人

foot-ahead no *man-eye*-see *ten-mouth*-ancient man

後不見來者

footstep-behind no *man-eye*-see *sprouting-wheat*-coming man

念天地之悠悠

heart-muse heaven earth of *heart*-expanse *heart*-expanse

獨愴然而涕下

dog-alone *heart*-woeful *water*-tear down

[DIAGNOSTIC TRANSLATION]

What's In English:

a- (ahead)

the

be- (behind)

-ing (coming, facing)

-ful (woeful)

-s (tears)

What's in Chinese:

州   (island)

口   (mouth)

不   (not)

目   (eye)

人   (man)

彳   (footstep)

來   (come)

心 , 卜   (heart)

天   (heaven)

土   (earth)

犭   (dog)

氵   (water)

下   (under)

PASSING THE HUAQING PALACE

Tu Mu

Piles of embroidery seen afar

from Chang'an,

mountain-top a thousand

gates open one by one.

A steed above the red dust,

a concubine smiling,

no one knows

it's the litchi coming.

Tu Mu (803-852). *Tang poet.*

The Huaqing Palace. A well-known entertainment place for Ming Emperor of Tang Dynasty and his concubine, Yang Guifei (a.k.a. Yang Kuei Fei). The latter almost brought the Dynasty to its ruin, and the Emperor was forced by his army to order her suicide.

Chang'an. The capital of the Tang Dynasty, now Xi'an in Shaanxi Province. The Huaqing Palace was situated to the west of Chang'an.

Litchi. A fruit grown in the south, and will rot very soon after being plucked. Since Yang Gui Fei was from the south and liked litchi, the Emperor set up a special express delivery route to send litchi by horses from the south to the Palace.

過華清宮
杜牧

長安回望繡成堆
山頂千門次第開
一騎紅塵妃子笑
無人知是荔枝來

[MORE EXPLANATIONS]

* Yang Gui Fei was the Yang Kuei-fei in William Carlos Williams'

"Prologue to *Kora in Hell*":

> But some have the power to free, say a young matron pursuing her
> infant, from her possessions, making her kin to Yang Kuei-fei
> because of a haunting loveliness that clings about her knees,
> impeding her progress as she takes up her matronly pursuit.

Only a few years later, Dr. Williams got himself drunk and drowned in the

fragrance of this ancient Oriental beauty again:

> In the spring I would drink! In the spring
> I would be drunk and lie forgetting all things.
> Your face! Give me your face, Yang Kue Fei!
> your hands, your lips to drink!
> Give me your wrists to drink--
> I drag you, I am drowned in you, you
> overwhelmed me! Drink!
> Save me! The shad bush is in the edge
> of the clearing. The yards in a fury
> of lilac blossoms are driving me mad with terror.
> Drink and lie forgetting the world.
>   --"Portrait of the Author"

3. 山 or 凵 (mountain). The peak on the top and a cave underneath.

3. 門 or 門 (door; gate). And,

開 or 闓 (open). Two hands pushing "open" the two door leaves.
From this line, 山頂千門次第開 (mountain-top a thousand gates

open one by one), we can see the visual syntactical flow of a Chinese poetry

line: "door" one by one "open."

4. 笑 or 笑 (smile). A human being (大) with two "smiling"

eyes (艸).

5. 無 or 森 (no; nothing). People are lost in the forest (*vide* "Rain

Bells" for further explanation).

[RADICAL TRANSLATION]

過華清宮

[Title] *Walk*-Pass Huaqing Palace

長安回望繡成堆

Chang'an back *full-moon*-look *silk*-embroidery pile *earth*-pile

山頂千門次第開

mountain *head*-top thousand door one by one *hands-push-door*-open

一騎紅塵妃子笑

one horse *silk*-red *deer*-dust *woman*-concubine child *man-eyes*-smile

無人知是荔枝來

people-lost-in-forest-no man *mouth*-know *sun-straight*-is *grass*-lit-*wood*-chi *sprouting-wheat*-come.

[DIAGNOSTIC TRANSLATION]

What's in English:

-ing (passing, smiling, coming)

the

-s (piles, gates)

-y (embroidery)

seen ("see")

a

-s (knows)

What's in Chinese:

辶 (walk)

月 (moon)

糸 (silk)

土 (earth)

山 (mountain)

頁 (head)

門 (door)

竹 (bamboo)

一 (one)

馬 (horse)

鹿 (deer)

女 (woman)

子 (child)

笑 (smile)

人 (man)

口 (mouth)

日 (sun)

艹 (grass)

木 (wood)

來 (come)

CHI-LE SONG

Anonymous

Chi-Le Plain

beneath Yin Mountain

sky like an arched tent

caging the wilderness

sky vast

wilderness boundless

wind blows, grass kotows,

   appear the cattle

Chi-Le Song. *A folk song of the Chi-Le Tribe, descedents of the Hun, who lived to the north of China, around the Mongolian grassland. This song was translated and collected during the Northern and Southern Dynasties (420-581).*

Arched tent. *Mongolian tent.*

Wilderness. *Originally "four wildernesses," the wilderness one sees in four directions*

敕勒歌

敕勒川
陰山下
天似穹廬
籠蓋四野
天蒼蒼
野茫茫
風吹草低見牛羊

42

[MORE EXPLANATIONS]

* A fact that can never be overemphasized but has nevertheless been readily neglected is that the classical "Chinese" literature borrowed in a large amount from other ethnic cultures. *Shi Jing* (*Book of Songs*), the first collection of Chinese poetry allegedly edited by Confucius, contains many folk songs which are not always "Chinese." *Yue Fu* (*Music Bureau*), folk ballads collected by the Bureau of Music of Han and the later dynasties (including the Southern and Northern Dynasties), also includes numerous folk songs/poems of the other ethnicities. Especially, the reason Chinese poetry has adopted strict metrical patterns is intimately related to the translations from the Sanskrit Buddhist texts. It was the encounter with an alphabetical language (Sanskrit) that had made the Chinese realize for the first time that a Chinese character was pronounced by a combination of vowel and consonant! But the canonical Chinese view has never been willing to recognize that the Middle Kingdom might not always be in the middle. Just like Mencius once said it without a wince: "I've heard of using the Xia (Chinese) to change the Yi (foreigners), but never heard of us being changed by them."

* Lin Yu-tang (1895-1976), the bilingual modern writer, wrote an American bestseller in 1935, *My Country and My People*. At one point in this book, Lin tried to explain the contrast between the sweets-eating southerners and horse-riding northerners:

> During the Southern Sung Dynasty, we saw a peculiar development of sentimental lyric in intricate meter, the *tz'u*, which invariably sang of the sad lady in her boudoir, and her tearful red candles at night and sweet-flavored rouge and eyebrow pencils, and silk curtains and beaded window screens and painted rails and departed springs, and pining lovers and emaciated sweethearts. It was natural that a people given to this kind of sentimental poetry should be conquered by a northern people who had but short, naive lines of poetry, taken, as it were, direct and without embellishment from the dreary northern landscape.

And what Lin gave as an example of such "short, naive lines of poetry" of the barbarous northern people was exactly this "Chi-Le Song"!

1. 歌 (song; sing). Two mouths (口) "singing."

2. 川 or 川川 (plain). Originally it is a picture of river (flowing water); the radical 氵 derives from this. Often 川 still means "river"; however, it refers to "plain" here. The etymology goes something like this: river --> river on a plain --> plain.

8. 牛 or 𐅂 (ox; cattle). An ox with two horns. Compare this with "sheep."

8. 羊 or 羊 (sheep). A sheep with two horns and four legs. A character derived from this, 樣 (model), was used by the early Jesuit missionaries as an example for the "universality" of Christianity. As their interpretation goes: this character is composed of 木 (wood cross) and 羊 (lamb); a lamb nailed onto a wood cross refers to Christ, a model. But the ancient version of 木 is 木 (upper branches, lower roots, and middle trunk -- an ideograph of tree), which is hardly the shape of a cross; other words which contain the "lamb" radical all seem to refer to the taste of mutton.

[RADICAL TRANSLATION]

敕勒歌

[Title] **Chi-Le** *Mouth-***Song**

敕勒川

Chi-Le *water-flowing-***plain**

陰山下

Yin Mountain under

天似穹廬

sky *man-***like** *hole-***arch** *roof-***tent**

籠蓋四野

*bamboo-***cage** *grass-***cover four wilderness**

天蒼蒼

sky *grass-***vast** *grass-***vast**

野茫茫

wilderness *grass-***boundless** *grass-***boundless**

風吹草低見牛羊

*worm-***wind** *mouth-***blow grass** *man-***low** *man-eye-***appear ox sheep**

[DIAGNOSTIC TRANSLATION]

What's in English:		*What's in Chinese:*	
the		口	(mouth)
an		川	(water, plain)
-ed (arched)		云	(cloud)
-ing (caging)		山	(mountain)
-s (blows, kotows)		下	(under)
-ness (wilderness)		亻	(man)
-less (boundless)		穴	(hole)
		弓	(arch)
		宀	(roof)
		竹	(bamboo)
		廿	(grass)
		天	(sky)
		虫	(worm)
		目	(eye)
		牛	(ox)
		羊	(sheep)

HEAVENLY CLEAR SAND:
AUTUMN THOUGHTS

Ma Zhi-Yuan

withered wisteria
    old trees
        crying crows
small bridge
    flowing water
        human house
ancient road
    west wind
        bony horse
sun setting
broken-hearted
    at sky's end

Ma Zhi-Yuan. Famous playwright of Yuan Dynasty (1271-1368), dates uncertain.

The transliteration of the poem is as follows, with the rhymes capitalized:

ku-teng lao-shu hun-YA
xiao-qiao liu-shui ren-JIA
gu-dao xi-feng shou-MA
xi-yang xi-XIA
duan-chang-ren zai tian-YA

Apparently, the first three lines are close to terza rima: each has three noun phrases, but no verb. Hence the three terze rime in English.

天淨沙

馬致遠

秋　思

枯藤老樹昏鴉。小橋流水人家。古道西風瘦馬。夕
陽西下,斷腸人在天涯　　。

[MORE EXPLANATIONS]

* The collaging of imagery in this poem, as in many other Chinese poems, is achieved by putting together noun phrases and leaving out all verbs, except in the last three lines, which have verbs, 下 (xia, set down), and

在 (zai, to be at). Such a non-sentence poetic syntax should be easily understandable from similar perspectives in Western poetry tradition, Impressionistic collage for one. Therefore, I would argue against many translators' practice of converting all Chinese poetry lines to full sentences.

* The most effective way Chinese poetry impresses a Western reader is through projecting itself as painted scenes which will eventually become "typically Chinese." Pearl S. Buck, an American writer steeped in Chinese literature, thus began her memoir, *My Several Worlds: A Personal Record*:

> This morning I rose early, as is my habit, and as usual I went to the open window and looked out over the land [at Green Hills Farm, Pennsylvania] that is to me the fairest I know. I see these hills and fields at dawn and dark, in sunshine and in moonlight, in summer green and winter snow, and yet there is always a new view before my eyes. Today, by the happy coincidence which seems the law of life, I looked at sunrise upon *a scene so Chinese* that I did not know I live on the other side of the globe, I might have believed it was from my childhood. A mist lay over the big pond under the weeping willows, a frail cloud, through which the water shone a silvered grey, and against this background stood a great white heron, profiled upon one stalk of leg. Centuries of Chinese artists have painted *that scene*.... (Emphasis mine)

Although Buck was describing a sunrise, it might be revealing to compare the images in her "a scene so Chinese" and the ones in Ma's poem.

* The last three lines are the so-called *qiangu juechang* (poetic masterpiece through the ages) because of the sentiments they embody in terse diction. Compare them with these lines from Pound's Cantos LXXIV:

> *Hooo Fasa, and in a dance the renewal*
> *with two larks in contrappunto*
> *at sunset*
> *ch'intenerisce*

The last Italian line ("that softens"), from Dante, depicts the "twilight hour softening the hearts of the homeward bound."

4. 家 or 家 (family; house). A pig is domesticated in a "house." An example of the Emersonian notion of poetry as "fossil language": the word itself documents early stages of human life. The failed 1970s Chinese Character Reformation changed the character to 穴 (a man in a house). But such a practice was rejected for not being "faithful" to the etymology of the word.

* Since the wording in this poem is so terse, I have taken some liberty to change a few things for the sake of poetic effect: withered wisteria (literally, "withered vines"); crying crows ("evening crows"); sun setting ("evening sun setting west").

[RADICAL TRANSLATION]

天淨沙

[Title] **Sky** *Water-***Clear** *Water-***Sand**

秋　思

[Subtitle] *Plant-Dry-***Autumn** *Heart-***Thought**

枯藤老樹昏鴉

*wood-***withered** *grass-***vine old** *wood-straight-***tree** *sun-set-***evening**
*bird-***crow**

小橋流水人家

small *wood-***bridge** *water-***flowing water man** *house-pig-***family**

古道西風瘦馬

*ten-mouth-***ancient** *walk-***road west** *worm-***wind** *sick-***bony horse**

夕陽西下

*moon-half-seen-***evening sun west down**

斷腸人在天涯

*blade-***cut** *meat-***bowel man** *earth-***at sky** *water-earth-***edge**

[DIAGNOSTIC TRANSLATION]

What's in English:

-ed (withered, broken-hearted)

-s (thoughts, trees, crows)

-ly (heavenly)

-ing (crying, flowing, setting)

-y (bony)

broken ("break")

What's in Chinese:

天 (sky)

氵 ，水 (water)

木 (wood)

艹 (grass)

日 (sun)

鳥 (bird)

人 (man)

宀 (house)

豕 (pig)

口 (mouth)

辶 (walk)

西 (west)

虫 (worm)

疒 (sick)

馬 (horse)

夕 (moon)

斤 (blade)

月 (meat)

土 (earth)

RAIN BELLS

Liu Yong

Cold cicadas creak.
Late at the pavilion,
shower's just stopped.
Tasteless drinks in the tent
    off the city gate,
where we linger,
the magnolia boat is urging us.
Holding hands, look into
    our tearing eyes,
words choked.
Thinking: this journey beyond
    thousands of miles
    of smoky waves,
evening mist so heavy
    under widening Chu sky.

The melancholic as ever
    grieves over departure,
let alone on this bleak
    Clear Autumn.
Tonight sober up where?
Willow banks, dawn breeze,
    waning moon.
This separation of years,
    pleasure hours, pleasing scenes
    shall all fall short.
My feelings
    of a thousand kind,
to whom can I spell?

Liu Yong (987?-1053?). The first professional Tz'u poet.

Pavilion. Ancient resting place by major routes.

Tasteless drinks. Because of the sadness of separation.

Chu. An ancient state in the south. So "Chu sky" means the "southern sky."

Clear Autumn. See the note in Li Po "Recollecting Chin-E."

Tonight...moon? I will sober from wine later, but where is it going to be? A vision of the bleak landscape.

雨霖鈴　　柳永

寒蟬淒切。對長亭晚，驟雨初歇。都門帳飲無緒，
留戀處，蘭舟催發。執手相看淚眼，竟無語凝噎。
念去去千里煙波，暮靄沈沈楚天闊。
多情自古傷離別，更那堪冷落清秋節。今宵酒醒何處？楊
柳岸，曉風殘月。此去經年，應是良辰好景虛設。便縱
有千種風情，更與何人說！

[MORE EXPLANATIONS]

5. 無 or 森 (no, without). Ernest Fenollosa in "The Chinese

Written Character as a Medium for Poetry" interprets this character as "to be

lost in the forest" and thereby makes his well-known point that Chinese

characters are close to nature and that nature does not contain negation:

> In nature there are no negations, no possible transfers of negative
> force. The presence of negative sentences in language would seem to
> corroborate the logicians' view that assertion is an arbitrary
> subjective act. *We* can assert a negation, though nature can not. But
> here again science comes to our aid against the logician: all
> apparently negative or disruptive movements bring into play other
> positive forces. It requires great effort to annihilate. Therefore we
> should suspect that, if we could follow back the history of all
> negative particles, we should find that they also are sprung from
> transitive verbs. It is too late to demonstrate such derivations in the
> Aryan languages, the clue has been lost; but in Chinese we can still
> watch positive verbal conceptions passing over into so-called
> negatives. Thus in Chinese the sign meaning "to be lost in the
> forest" relates to a state of non-existence. English "not"= the
> Sanskrit *na*, which may come from the root *na*, to be lost, to perish.

1. 雨 (rain). — is sky; | , vapors rising from the earth. ∶∶ , rain drops falling.

7. 舟 or 𣶒 (boat).

8. 手 or 𠂸 (hand).

15. 醒 (sobering up from wine). The radical, 酉 , or 西 , is the ancient character for wine (an ideograph of wine vessel). Later 氵 (water) was added to indicate "wine." 醒 , because of the "wine" radical, used to only mean "waking up from wine"; later the meaning is extended to "wake up" in general.

19. 有 (to have; there to be). Again it's an example used by Fenollosa in the essay to indicate the concreteness of the Chinese:

> In Chinese the chief verb for 'is' not only means actively 'to have,' but shows by its derivation that it expresses something even more
>
> concrete, namely 'to snatch from the moon with the hand.' 有
>
> Here the baldest symbol of prosaic analysis is transformed by magic into a splendid flash of concrete poetry.

[RADICAL TRANSLATION]

雨霖鈴

[Title] **Rain** *Endless*-**Rain** *Metal*-**Bell**

寒蟬淒切

cold *insect*-**cicada** *water*-**chill** *blade*-**cut**

對長亭晚

face long pavilion *sun*-**late**

驟雨初歇

horse-**sudden rain just stop**

都門帳飲無緒

city gate *cloth*-**tent drink** *people-lost-in-forest*-**no** *silk*-**thread**

留戀處

stay *heart*-**love place**

蘭舟催發

grass-**magnolia boat** *man*-**urge start**

執手相看淚眼

hold hand *eye-each-other* *eye-***look** *water-***tear eye**

竟無語凝噎

but *people-lost-in-forest-***no** *mouth-***word congeal** *mouth-***choke**

念去去

*heart-***think go go**

千里煙波

thousand mile *fire-***smoke** *water-skin-***wave**

莽靄沈沈楚天闊

*sun-grass-***dusk** *rain-***mist** *water-***sink** *water-***sink Chu sky** *gate-***wide**

多情自古傷離別

many *heart-***emotion from** *ten-mouth-***ancient** *man-***hurt** *bird-***leave**
*bone-blade-***separate**

更那堪冷落清秋節

*sun-***more how** *earth-***endure cold** *grass-***fall** *Water-***Clear** *Plant-Dry-***
Autumn** *bamboo-***festival**

今宵酒醒何處

this night *water*-wine *wine*-wake *man*-what place

楊柳岸曉風殘月

wood-yang *wood*-willow *mountain*-bank *sun*-dawn *worm*-wind
handicap moon

此去經年

this go *silk*-many year

應是良辰好景虛設

heart-should *sun*-straight-is nice moment *woman-child*-good *sun*-
scene empty *word*-set

便縱有千種風情

man-even if *hand-snatch-from-moon*-have thousand *plant*-sort
worm-wind *heart*-emotion

更與何人說

sun-more with *man*-who man *word*-speak

[DIAGNOSTIC TRANSLATION]

What's in English:

-s (bells, cicadas, drinks, hands, eyes,

    words, thousands, waves, banks,

    years, hours, scenes, feelings)

-s (grieves)

the

-ed (stopped, choked)

-ing (urging, holding, tearing, thinking

    widening, waning, pleasing)

-less (tasteless)

a

-y (smoky)

to- (tonight)

whom ("who")

What's in Chinese:

雨 (rain)

金 (metal)

虫 (insect)

氵 (water)

刀 , 刂 (blade)

日 (sun)

馬 (horse)

門 (door)

巾 (cloth)

無 (no)

糸 (silk)

心 , 忄 (heart)

艹 (grass)

舟 (boat)

亻 (man)

手 (hand)

目 (eye)

口 (mouth)

火 (fire)

禾 (plant)

月 , 夕 (moon)

鳥 (bird)

竹 (bamboo)

土 (earth)

酉 (wine)

木 (wood)

山 (mountain)

女 (woman)

子 (child)

有 (have)

言 (word)

WEI CITY TUNE

Wang Wei

Wei City's dawn rain

    wets the light dust

the guest-inn greens with

    the new willow hue

why not drink

    one more round

west of Yang Gate

    no friend to be found

Wang Wei (701-761). Well-known for the simple, natural style of his poems.

Wei City. To the northwest of today's Xi'an (i.e. Chang'an), an ancient capital now famous for its "Terra-Cotta Warriors."

Yang Gate. A key pass on the Silk Road and the route to the northwest borders.

渭城曲

王維

渭城朝雨浥輕塵
客舍青青柳色新
勸君更盡一杯酒
西出陽關無故人

[MORE EXPLANATIONS]

* In *Cathay* (1915), Ezra Pound used this poem as an epigraph for the "Four Poems of Departure" by Rihaku (Li Po). Pound's version reads:

Light rain is on the light dust.
The willow of the inn-yard
Will be going greener and greener,
But you, Sir, had better take wine ere your departure,
For you will have no friends about you
When you come to the gates of Go.

The word "Go," despite its alliteration with "gates," is Pound's misreading of Fenollosa's cursive "Yo," which is the Japanese pronunciation of the Chinese character 陽 (Yang).

2. 輕 (light). It originally refers to "light carriage." The radical on the left, 車 , is a picture of a carriage looked at from the side, 🎑 (the two strokes on both sides are wheels).

3. 舍 or 㐖 (house). A picture of a house with the roof on the top.

3. 青 or 𤯎 (blue; green). Wood on fire, causing "blue" flame. Pound's rendition, following Fenollosa's transcription, therefore has its justification, although the character means "green" here.

4. 盡 (empty). The lower radical 𤇾 , or 🏵 , is a vessel. The vessel is "empty."

5. 西 or 𠧋 (west). It's a bird sitting on its nest--time to rest; therefore, the sun must be in the "west." The opposite of 東 (east)--the sun just rises among the branches.

[RADICAL TRANSLATION]

渭城曲
[Title] **Wei City Tune**

渭城朝雨浥輕塵
Wei City *sun-moon-*dawn **rain wet** *carriage-***light** *deer-***dust**

客舍青青柳色新
*house-***guest house** *wood-flame-***blue** *wood-flame-***blue** *wood-***willow color** *wood-blade-***new**

勸君更盡一杯酒
*force-***persuade** *mouth-respect-***you** *ṣun-***more** *vessel-***empty one** *wood-***cup** *water-***wine**

西出陽關無故人
*bird-on-nest-***west** *plant-***come-out Yang Gate** *people-lost-in-forest-***no** *ten-mouth-***old man**

[DIAGNOSTIC TRANSLATION]

What's in English:

's (Wei City's)
-s (wets, greens)
the
found ("find")

What's in Chinese:

氵 (water)
土 (earth)
日 (sun)
月 (moon)
雨 (rain)
車 (carriage)
鹿 (deer)
馬 (house)
青 (blue)
木 (wood)
斤 (blade)
口 (mouth)
皿 (vessel)
一 (one)
酉 (wine)
西 (west)
來 (come out)
門 (gate)
無 (no)
人 (man)

WATER TUNE PRELUDE

Su Shi

*Su Shi (1036-
1101). A Sung
literary giant
famed for the
unrestrainedness
of his poetry.*

*Preface: The Mid-Autumn Festival of 1076, happy
drinking till dawn, very drunk, composing this piece
also to express thoughts of my brother Zi You.*

When shall the moon shine again?
Holding the wine, asking the sky.
Wonder what year it is now,
       in Heavenly Palace.
I'd ride on wind and return,
but afraid of
       the jasper towers and jade houses,
       too high in the unbearable chill.
Rise to dance with my bleak shadow,
what a human world!

*Heavenly Palace.
The palace of the
Jade Emperor in
heaven,
consisting of the
"jasper towers
and jade
houses."*

Turning round the red pavilion,
declining to the latticed window,
shining on the sleepless.
No grudge should be held,
but why always wax in time of separation?
Man knows sorrow, joy, part, union;
moon knows cloudy, clear, wax, wane:
perfect it is never.
But would all live as ever,
sharing this moon a thousand miles apart.

*Turning...sleep-
less. Describes
the movement of
the moon.*

*No...separation.
"I" shouldn't
complain against
the moon, but
why is it always
full at the wrong
time?*

水調歌頭

蘇軾

丙辰中秋, 歡飲達旦, 大醉, 作此篇,
兼懷子由。
明月幾時有? 把酒問青天。不知天上宮闕, 今夕
是何年。我欲乘風歸去, 惟恐瓊樓玉宇, 高處不勝寒。起
舞弄清影, 何似在人間。　　轉朱閣, 低綺戶, 照無眠。
不應有恨, 何事長向別時圓? 人有悲歡離合, 月有陰晴圓
缺, 此事古難全。但願人長久, 千里共嬋娟。

[MORE EXPLANATIONS]

2. 明 or 🌙 (shine; bright). A classic example of the "vividness" of the Chinese character: "sun" and "moon" together to indicate shining.

3. 把 or 𢪘 (hold). It can't be more wrong to assume that all Chinese characters are hieroglyphic. Like in this word, the radical on the left is pictorially "hand," but the right part is simply the pronunciation of the word "ba." Therefore this character is a combination of sound and picture.

5. 夕 or 𝄅 (night). The moon half seen.

6. 我 (I; myself). The left-side "hand" holding a right-side "weapon" (defending "myself").

7. 玉 or 王 (jade). Three pieces of jade linked by a string in the middle.

8. 寒 or  (cold; chill). Three people under the roof, covered by grass (hays) to keep themselves from the "cold."

9. 影 (shadow). The left side, 景 or , is "sunshine." The right side, 彡 , indicates the "shade" or "shadow."

10. 閒 or  (between). It is a moon seen "between" two door leaves. For this meaning this character is usually written as 間 . 人間 means "the human world" ("between" human beings). This character can also mean "leisure" (having the "leisure" time to watch the moon shine through your door). Therefore, in *Fir-Flower Tablets*, *Amy* Lowell and Florence Ayscough rendered this character into a phrase: "And calm with the leisure of moonlight through an open door."

15. 別 or  (separate). Cut the bone,  , with a knife,  .

[RADICAL TRANSLATION]

水調歌頭

[Title] **Water** *Word*-**Tune** *Mouth*-**Song Head**

明月幾時有

sun-moon-**bright moon what** *sun*-**time** *hand-snatch-from-moon*-**have**

把酒問青天

hand-**hold** *water*-**wine** *mouth*-**ask** *wood-flame*-**blue sky**

不知天上宮闕

not *mouth*-**know sky above** *roof*-**palace** *door*-**palace**

今夕是何年

this *moon-half-seen*-**night** *sun-straight*-**is** *man*-**what year**

我欲乘風歸去

hand-hold-weapon-**I desire ride** *worm*-**wind return gone**

惟恐瓊樓玉宇

just *heart*-**afraid jasper** *wood*-**tower jade** *roof*-**house**

高處不勝寒

high place not *meat*-endure cold

起舞弄清影

step-rise dance play *water-blue*-bleak *sunshine*-shadow

何似在人間

man-how *man*-like *earth*-in man *moon-through-door*-between

轉朱閣

carriage-turn red *door*-pavilion

低綺戶

man-low *silk*-lattice window

照無眠

sun-shine *people-lost-in-forest*-no *eye*-sleep

不應有恨

not *heart*-should *hand-snatch-from-moon*-have *heart*-grudge

何事長向別時圓
man-**what matter long** *window-open-***toward** *bone-blade*-**separate**
sun-**time round**

人有悲歡離合
man *hand-snatch-from-moon*-**have** *heart*-**sorrow** *bird*-**happy** *bird*-
separate *mouth*-**union**

月有陰晴圓缺
moon *hand-snatch-from-moon*-**have cloudy** *sun*-**clear round lack**

此事古難全
this matter *ten-mouth*-**ancient** *bird*-**difficult complete**

但願人長久
man-**only** *head*-**wish man long long**

千里共嬋娟
thousand li share *woman*-**beauty** *woman*-**beauty**

70

[DIAGNOSTIC TRANSLATION]

What's in English:

-ing (drinking, composing, shining,
    holding, asking, turning,
    declining, sharing)

a

the

drunk ("drink")

-s (thoughts, towers, houses, miles)

-ed (latticed)

-less (sleepless)

-s (knows)

a- (apart)

What's in Chinese:

水 ， 氵 (water)

口 (mouth)

頁 (head)

日 (sun)

月 ， 夕 (moon)

有 (have)

才 (hand)

酉 (wine)

青 (blue)

天 (sky)

不 (not)

上 (above)

宀 (roof)

門 (door)

亻 (man)

我 (I)

虫 (worm)

心 ， 小 (heart)

玉 (jade)

木 (wood)

寒 (cold)

走 (step)

影 (shadow)
閒 (between)
車 (carriage)
糸 (silk)
戶 (window)
無 (no)
目 (eye)
何 (toward)
刂 (blade)
隹 (bird)
女 (woman)

ROOF BOOKS (Partial List)

Andrews, Bruce. **EX WHY ZEE**. 112p. $10.95.

Andrews, Bruce. **Getting Ready To Have Been Frightened**. 116p. $7.50.

Benson, Steve. **Blue Book**. Copub. with The Figures. 250p. $12.50

Bernstein, Charles. **Islets/Irritations**. 112p. $9.95.

Bernstein, Charles (editor). **The Politics of Poetic Form**. 246p. $12.95; cloth $21.95.

Brossard, Nicole. **Picture Theory**. 188p. $11.95.

Child, Abigail. **Scatter Matrix**. 79p. $9.95.

Davies, Alan. **Active 24 Hours**. 100p. $5.

Davies, Alan. **Signage**. 184p. $11.

Davies, Alan. **Rave**. 64p. $7.95.

Day, Jean. **A Young Recruit**. 58p. $6.

Di Palma, Ray. **Motion of the Cypher**. 112p. $10.95.

Di Palma, Ray. **Raik**. 100p. $9.95.

Doris, Stacy. **Kildare**. 104p. $9.95.

Dreyer, Lynne. **The White Museum**. 80p. $6.

Edwards, Ken. **Good Science**. 80p. $9.95.

Eigner, Larry. **Areas Lights Heights**. 182p. $12, $22 (cloth).

Gizzi, Michael. **Continental Harmonies**. 92p. $8.95.

Gottlieb, Michael. **Ninety-Six Tears**. 88p. $5.

Grenier, Robert. **A Day at the Beach**. 80p. $6.

Grosman, Ernesto. **The XUL Reader: An Anthology of Argentine Poetry (1981–1996)**. 167p. $14.95.

Hills, Henry. **Making Money**. 72p. $7.50. VHS videotape $24.95. Book & tape $29.95.

Hunt, Erica. **Local History**. 80 p. $9.95.

Inman, P. **Criss Cross**. 64 p. $7.95.

Inman, P. **Red Shift**. 64p. $6.

Lazer, Hank. **Doublespace**. 192 p. $12.

Mac Low, Jackson. **Representative Works: 1938–1985**. 360p. $12.95, $18.95 (cloth).

Mac Low, Jackson. **Twenties**. 112p. $8.95.

Moriarty, Laura. **Rondeaux**. 107p. $8.

Neilson, Melanie. **Civil Noir**. 96p. $8.95.

Pearson, Ted. **Planetary Gear**. 72p. $8.95.

Perelman, Bob. **Virtual Reality**. 80p. $9.95.

Piombino, Nick, **The Boundary of Blur**. 128p. $13.95.

Raworth, Tom. **Clean & Will-Lit**. 106p. $10.95.

Robinson, Kit. **Balance Sheet**. 112p. $9.95.

Robinson, Kit. **Ice Cubes**. 96p. $6.

Scalapino, Leslie. **Objects in the Terrifying Tense Longing from Taking Place**. 88p. $9.95.

Seaton, Peter. **The Son Master**. 64p. $5.

Sherry, James. **Popular Fiction**. 84p. $6.

Silliman, Ron. **The New Sentence**. 200p. $10.

Silliman, Ron. **N/O**. 112p. $10.95.

Templeton, Fiona. **Cells of Release**. 128p. with photographs. $13.95.

Templeton, Fiona. **YOU—The City**. 150p. $11.95.

Ward, Diane. **Human Ceiling**. 80p. $8.95.

Ward, Diane. **Relation**. 64p. $7.50.

Watten, Barrett. **Progress**. 122p. $7.50.

Weiner, Hannah. **We Speak Silent**. 76 p. $9.95

Discounts (same title): 1 – 4 books—20%; 5 or more—40%. .(Postage 4th Class incl., UPS extra)
For complete list or ordering, send check or money order in U.S. dollars to:
SEGUE FOUNDATION, 303 East 8th Street, New York, NY 10009